Boring The Arse
Off Young People

Martin Figura

To Jo

Best wishes

[signature]

June 2014
Wakefield.

Nasty Little Press

Published by Nasty Little Press in November 2010.
Reprinted in 2011, 2012.

Nasty Little Press
35 St Johns Road, Bungay, Suffolk

nastylittlepress.org

Printed and bound by Print2Demand Ltd
17 Burgess Road, Ivyhouse Lane, Hastings, East Sussex.

ISBN: 978-0-9563767-3-2

A CIP record of this book is available
from the British Library.

Nasty Little Press is the proud recipient of a Grants for the Arts
Award from Arts Council England.

LOTTERY FUNDED

for Lilly Figura
born 29 May 2009

Acknowledgements

Acknowledgements are due to the editor of this collection Sally Roe.

Special thanks also to Luke Wright and Helen Ivory.

'Ahem' previously appeared in the book of the same title published by Egg Box Publishing as did '(The Trouble With) Middle Aged People' and 'Family Chirstmas.' 'Ahem' also appeared in *The Rialto*. 'Acrostic' appeared in the Gatehouse Press anthology *Gift*. 'This Be The Worst' was first published in *The Little Book of Harm* (Firewater Press).

Contents

Published

The local bookshop said
they'd take one for now.

It stood thinly on the shelf
between all of Eliot

and
all of Heaney.

Dear Mr and Mrs Ainscough

you have nothing to worry about: house prices are not affected
by wheelie-bins; Princess Diana's death was an accident;
Muslims have the same wheelie-bins as everyone else;
there is no need for Mr Ainscough to watch your wheelie-bin
from quite so early in the morning, as only milkmen (and
Mr Ainscough) are up at that time; Jonathan Ross is leaving
Radio 2, unfortunately he is being replaced by yet another
homosexual; wheelie bins are made in Britain; single-mothers
are not given priority for new wheelie-bins; wheelie-bins are no
where gangsta-rappers hide their guns; Health & Safety
has fallen down a hole; under the Freedom of Information Act
we can tell you that there is one bobby on the beat for every
two hundred and twenty seven wheelie-bins, an increase
of 10% since the last election; intelligence reports show
al-Qaeda consider Wingfield Avenue not a high enough
profile target to use your wheelie-bin as a bomb; Bill Nighy
is delighted Mrs Ainscough finds him dishy; teenage boys
have been told to pull their trousers up and wear their hats
the right way round; it is unlikely that an artist will steal
your wheelie-bin for an installation; this problem is confined
to Hoxton; even young people find Bono annoying; your
wheelie-bin does not need to be melted down for the war
in Afghanistan; there are no plans to change the colour
of wheelie-bins because they are black; life does mean life;
your wheelie-bin will continue to be emptied every week.

A Northern Accent

Having moved south, it's not something
you're going to need all the time.
Keep it about your person though,
for those occasions when it can
do you some good. For instance:
making southerners feel as if
they haven't worked quite as hard
as they might have to get where they are.
Use it to order beer, but not wine.
And when you meet a real northerner
keep your mouth shut.

Talking

I just talk too much I talk too much
never shut up if you cut me in half
with a spade I'd continue to talk
for up to nearly an hour from both ends
I'm more send than receive have never
had an unexpressed thought in my life
the path behind me is littered
with the hind legs of donkeys
those times when you should just shut up
that's when I talk even more let it tumble out
no matter how incriminating
there would be no need to tie me to a chair
and slap a rubber hose into the palm of your hand
for I will sing like a canary at the politest enquiry
tell you more about myself then you ever wanted to know
give up my own children just for a chat
in fact I can guarantee that the most hardened torturer
will soon be sewing up my mouth
to stop me telling him what I know
but I shall only rip my mouth open
spit out my broken teeth and carry on talking
through my tattered bleeding lips
and what I don't know I don't let worry me
for I never let lack of knowledge get in the way
of giving an opinion why should I

I've a habit of repeating myself
I've a habit of repeating myself
that was pretty obvious right,
but you try talking non-stop
and not saying something pretty obvious along the way
and if you're one of those quiet people that just looks
then you're just asking for it without actually asking
if you see what I mean but you can't just stand
and look at each other right
and if *you're* not going to say something then I have to
simple as that simple as that so it's your own fault
don't glaze over when I'm talking to you
if you want this poem to stop sometime
in the next hour then for God's sake
do something useful
go and fetch a spade.

The Grey Eye

This box of tricks,
static witch, begetter
of dust, one-eyed
watcher of sofas,
one-eyed watcher
of us, mirror of us,
a better future, a cure
for dandruff, brighter stuff,
bringer of America,
transmitter of smut,
the only flicker of life
in the front-room tonight,
every night.

We praise you
we praise you
bring us recipes
bring us happiness
and bring us soap
give us a reason for next week
and give us life
and give us reality
O make us over
give us light.

And may all our cops
be maverick cops,
and our antiques
be our fortune,
show us a lioness
rip the throat
from a deer
as we peel the lids
from our take-aways.

Bring us the best
one hundred nights in
ever,
we thank you
we praise you
we thank you
Amen.

Acrostic

Now the birds sing
I am gifted each
Clear note
Epiphany

The start of each day
Is your song, your scent
This heaven
Sweet and sure.

Still

Tell me who's to say what beautiful is,
who's to say what beautiful is, when
I've come this distance, fifty years, fifty years
putting flesh on these bones, putting flesh
on these bones like wisdom? And who's to say
I shouldn't dance, when this baby just wants
to dance, loves to dance, loves to let this midriff
sway, sway and flow until my shirt becomes
an ocean, until my heat soaks it through, until it
clings, then let it shine, let it shine in the disco lights,
let it shine blue and gold and who's to say
I shouldn't love, and who's to say I shouldn't love
so give me lord someone to hold, and gone
are the days when we must grope in the darkness,
gone are the days when we must grope in the darkness,
leave the lights on, leave the lights on and look and look
and sing vol – upt – uous, babeee, vol – upt – uous and then
we'll touch, and kiss and touch and heave ourselves
together and no-one's going to stop us doing
what we want to, no-one's going to stop us doing
what we want to, we'll keep this flesh moving,
we'll keep this flesh moving, and when we've finished
doing what we want to, this flesh will keep moving still,
this flesh will keep moving still, this flesh will keep moving
                                                    still.

I Don't Know Where It All Went Wrong,
But My Life's Turned Into a Tom Waits Song

I'm stuck in this college town full of those bright shiny kids
that are there just to make you feel bad about yourself
and my job is putting feathers and chicken shit
onto supermarket barn eggs and the couple next door
are going for some kind of record and there's a man
nailed to a piece of wood on my wall who looks like
he might understand.

I head to the diner with my friend Tom, Tom's
got a metal plate in his head that picks up
the country music station when the weather's right.
                              Tom hates country music.
He got married once, found out on his wedding night
his wife was a man. He's given up on romance now,
says that's not the kinda thing you want to see
hanging out of the bottom of a negligee
                              twice in your life.

And the diner is this gumball place full of broken-hearted
insomniacs, the coffee's bitter and who can blame it
and the waitress is called Maria, she has been-to-bed eyes
and ramshackle breasts that don't seem related, they just kind of

swim around in there, bouncing off each other, its hard
to take your eyes off 'em. When she takes her teeth out
she can suck the cork from a bottle of wine,
                                we drink a lot of wine.

In the morning a hefty dwarf sits on my chest, beats my head
with his wooden leg, hands me a cigarette and a Coca-Cola
flips a coin, sets the television set on fire and leaves
with my dog Pete. The disc jockey on the radio
says it's another rainy day outside, so you look
and sure enough, it's another rainy day outside.

America, We Love You Here in England

It seems every time I turn on the TV
someone's running you guys down
calling you oppressors and suchlike
when all you're trying to do is help.
You know we're on board, right?
You speak our language, or kind of.
Gee, you've probably improved it.
Glitzed it up a whole bunch.

As a thank you I went down to the park
(we have parks too, not as big as your parks,
no geysers or canyons, grand or otherwise,
but we still call them parks, if that's ok)
and I wrote this poem. It's kind of like
a Randy Newman song
only not as good.

Once we were oppressors too, so they say.
And just to warn you, these people have long memories
hundreds of years from now they'll keep bringing it up:
you know, the conquering, the famines and slaughter.
Our closest neighbours seem to hate us most of all.
Do you find that? How are those Canadians treating you?
Do they always cheer for the other team?

We owned you a long time ago,
but you don't keep bitching about it.
America, you seem to love us
and we love you right back.
You've sent us Madonna
and we sent you Simon Cowell;
these people are fine ambassadors.

You've got a new fella in charge now.
He seems a nice guy, handsome too.
The Queen is getting tired, and Charles,
well, Charles just isn't King material.
Maybe Obama would like to step up
and wear the crown for a while? I know
his folks had a little trouble with us
in Kenya, but hey, that's all in the past.

We've got history that goes way back:
palaces, castles, all kinds of quaint old shit
that you like. Come on over,
make yourself at home.
Tell them I said it was ok.

If I Was Irish, I Would Write Helen Ivory a Love Poem

I would so
for she is a magnificent woman
is she not?
She has a fine pair of shoulders on her
and would have no trouble
carrying buckets.
And is her skin not as soft as Donegal rain
and her eyes as misty and deep
as Lough Corrib in County Galway?
And sure her voice is sweeter than all the lullabies.
Does her laugh not bring to mind
what it must have been like to hear
the 4ᵗʰ Royal Irish Dragoon Guards
crossing a tin bridge on their horses?
And she has one hell of a backside on her
so she does.
As ornate as the balcony
of the Grand Opera House up in Belfast there.
I could not be doing with those *fashion* girls
with no hips to speak of, or breasts.
LET ME TELL YOU HELEN IVORY HAS BREASTS
O YES! A good man could get happily lost in those breasts
as comforting as feather pillows they are.

And she has hips too
hips you can get hold of
so you can pull her close
and smell her hair, which is a bit mad
but smells of meadows and fresh air.

But I'm not Irish so I don't know what to say
in the face of such magnificence.
It's not that being English I don't have the words
sure, I just don't have the extravagance.

Norwich, Midnight

Sensing somehow earthquake or fire
creatures scurry through Mousehold Heath.
The moon snags on the cathedral's spire
as we walk home down Magdalen Street;

through the inner ring road underpass
the piss-yellow glow of the Oxfam shop,
in whose doorway we stop and kiss
kebabs in hand, with greasy chops.

Anglia Square has never looked so beautiful
littered as she is with burger boxes.
Praise the Lord and the City Council
down from the Heath come the urban foxes.

Break Up Dream

Did you have to be so honest when I asked you for the truth
then place me here so short of breath
displayed upon the Town Hall steps
wearing just this tiny vest
to cover up my modesty
while you tip my shopping out
all my various chemistry
purple pills that help men pee
scatter out across the street
you squeeze the creams for my skin diseases
into the bag where my favourite cheese is
Jesus this is where the hurt is
the Market Place where love is bartered
the Market Place where I'm now martyred
the Market Place I try to run from
the Market Place my feet won't shift from
where my visage is a gurning grimace
and you shout *LOOK that's his sex face!*
then the crowd join in and chant it
SEX FACE SEX FACE SEX FACE
while I'm led away in my little vest
my privates hide in a policeman's helmet
while you have somehow found a bell
and like a crier bellow out
LADIES AND GENTLEMEN A SMALL HELMET
A VERY SMALL HELMET INDEED.

Waiting for Lilly
b 29 May 2009

Lilly, this is the second weekend in a row
we have waited, texting each other for news
while you simply refuse to show yourself.
Today is a bank holiday Sunday, the hottest day
of the year so far. Your poor mother is stuck
in her tiny flat with her bag packed and her back
aching, while your father, who can do nothing right,
is smoking guiltily on the balcony. Your grandmother,
my ex-wife, is a woman of action and if she doesn't
have things and people to organise
very soon, we are all going to suffer.

I'm not sure you realise, but I have a very full week
and driving to Cambridge, will be, to say the least
inconvenient (unless it's Thursday, when I have
a meeting there). But I shall do it on whatever day,
because I must, and if necessary the board of directors
can wait for their end of year report, because you, Lilly,
are more important.

I can perhaps understand your reluctance.
I think its fair to say that our family
has not always covered itself in glory,
and the world outside is a mess.

Politicians and bankers are in disgrace,
policemen are clubbing people in the street,
even the new Professor of Poetry at Oxford
was asked to stand down after less than a week.
We are involved in at least two wars that I know about.

Do you realise that at your eighteenth birthday party
I shall be seventy years old, if I last that long?
I'm not saying this is your fault – but in a way it is –
that's how life works: one in, one out.
The best I can hope for now is a little
overlap. If I do make it, and you invite me,
I shall be in the corner reminiscing, handing out
pearls of wisdom that are neither wanted or wise,
worse still I shall dance to whatever passes
for music in 2027 and I shall probably smell a bit.

So, Lilly, a clean white sheet awaits, and you should try
not to worry about the weight of responsibility, but focus
on becoming a chatterbox. Knowing your mother
this should not be a problem. We will allow you a few sulks
during the awkward years, but overall we shall expect you
to be sweet.

This Be The Worst

They fuck you up, your kids
they may not mean to, but they do.
They take all the faults you have
and throw them back, twice as hard at you.

But they will fuck up in their turn
with fashionable clothes that look good now
but in years to come, in a photograph album,
will return to shame and haunt them.

Children return love as guilt to parents
that deepens like crap on a bedroom floor.
Move them on as early as you can
and don't ever try for any more.

(The Trouble With) Middle Aged People

Middle aged people today don't know they're born.
What do they think they're up to?
They should be occupying their time with:
> jigsaws,
> the litter problem,
> gravy,
> coach trips to The Norfolk Lavender Fields.

But no, they're at Glastonbury,
boring the arse off young people
about Dylan or how they saw The Who
in their heyday in '68, doing degrees
with no possible practical application,
motorcycling across India to *find* themselves.

There's even one reading you this poem, and look
he's wearing red trainers with white stripes.

Fifty

Any day now,
my libido
will slip on
its knapsack
and old
turtle-neck
sweater
and slouch
off
over
the hill.

Family Christmas

Every single year
we gather around the tree
opening old wounds.

AHEM

After Ginsberg

I saw the best suits of my parents' generation
    destroyed by poor tailoring, synthetic fibres
    and hysterical lapels,
dragging their shopping down the high streets
    of Albion in pacamacs with hairdos under
    hairnets and headscarves,
Brylcreem-headed husbands burning pipe tobacco
    in walnut bowls and inhaling through
    the clenched teeth of repressed ardour,
who feared the wind rush in the negro streets
    of Victoriana blowing the sounds and smells
    that threaten the unfamiliar and didn't
    even know Elvis Presley existed yet,
who got drunk on home-made egg-flip at Christmas
    and sang the old songs around the piano
    while their kids were happy with a tangerine
    and Dinky Toy,
who saved so that one day they might have
    a little car and be saluted by the AA man
    as they drove by,
who were all the time boiling vegetables to eat with
    Spam while listening to the radiogram valves
    singing hot with Family Favourites and after sprouts
    there was Much Binding in The Marsh until

Billy Cotton cried out WAKEY WAKEY and
Bandstand glowed out in the deathly grey
of cathode rays,
who on Fridays went dancing up the club in sixpence
a week Montague Burton suits and crammed into
eighteen hour girdles and mail order dresses with
their blue hair piled on top, but just too soon
to have been teenagers,
who tripped out to Skegness Vimto-fuelled in charabancs
to shine under Billy Butlin's neon "Our true intent is all
for your delight" while being served brown ale by lasses
from Doncaster in grass skirts under plastic palm trees
in The Beachcomber Bar,
who never used the front room but kept it pure and the
antimacassars pressed for visits by doctors or
vicars or teachers for tinned salmon and tinned pears
and tinned milk and polished their front steps
and never ran out of string,
who knew their place and never thought the universities
were for the likes of them, but prayed for office jobs
for their children and stood for God Save The Queen
at the Empire and said how wonderful their policemen
were and fought in the war for the likes of me,
who had more words for toilet than the Inuit have for snow
and put their teeth in jars then slept in their vests
under candlewick counterpanes in cold bedrooms
with dreams of winning the pools and bungalows
in Cheshire with inside loos and labour saving devices,

who at dawn trod into brown slippers onto cold brown
linoleum and could only face the day through the
sweet brown haze of a hundred cups of tea and
twenty Capstan Full Strength.

Also by NASTY LITTLE PRESS

High Performance
by Luke Wright
ISBN: 978-0-9563767-0-1 | £5

What If Men Burst In Wearing Balaclavas?
by John Osborne
ISBN: 978-0-9563767-1-8 | £5

Barking Doggerel
by Byron Vincent
ISBN: 978-0-9563767-2-5 | £5

www.nastylittlepress.org